IDAHO
portrait of a state

"**TWIN LAKES** at right are in Jewel Basin. The fuzzy white puffs are bear grass blossoms. They remind me of tiny polar bears."

Montana

"**AN OLD HOUSE** still stands along Grave Creek near Eureka on the Canadian border."

BRILLIANT LEAVES of this cottonwood remind me that fall is just around the corner."

have gone with the flow of Missouri River. Don't ask m choose a favorite region... would be like asking a chil choose which parent or gra parent he liked best.

I came to Montana as a dent 22 years ago. I never le figure once you find *"God's Ct try"*, why not just stay put?

Coming Up Next: Jean F will take you on a photo-tou the Shenandoah Valley of ginia. She feels it's absolutely

IDAHO

portrait of a state

MARK LISK

GRAPHIC ARTS BOOKS

Library of Congress Control Number: 2007929887
International Standard Book Number: 978-0-88240-694-7

Captions and book compilation © MMVII by
Graphic Arts Books, an imprint of
Graphic Arts Center Publishing Company
P.O. Box 10306, Portland, Oregon 97296-0306
503/226-2402; www.gacpc.com

The five-dot logo is a registered trademark of
Graphic Arts Center Publishing Company.

President: Charles M. Hopkins
Associate Publisher: Douglas A. Pfeiffer
Editorial Staff: Timothy W. Frew, Kathy Howard, Jean Bond-Slaughter
Production Coordinators: Heather Doornink, Vicki Knapton
Cover Design: Elizabeth Watson
Interior Design: Jean Andrews

Printed in China

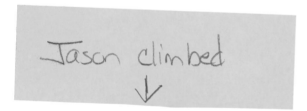

FRONT COVER: ◖ Old Hyndman Peak, 11,887 feet
high, rises above Wild Horse Lake in the Pioneer Mountains.
BACK COVER: ◖ Sulfur paintbrush *(Castilleja sulphurea)* flowers
flourish along the bank of Bear Valley Creek in the Boise National Forest.
◀◀ Penstemon, trumpet-shaped blossoms arranged around a central spike,
blooms on the massive granite boulders above Pistol Creek Rapid on the
Middle Fork of the Salmon River. Penstemon comes in a variety of colors.
◀ Boulder Lake serves as mirror for the peaks of the Pioneer Range.
▶ Brilliant orange light reflects from Lake Lucille in the Sawtooth
Wilderness, which encompasses more than two hundred
thousand acres managed by the U.S. Forest Service.

◄ Aspens in fall foliage accent the rocky
terrain in the Boulder Mountains of central Idaho.
▲ The Teton Basin shows just a microcosm of the nearly twelve
million acres of farmland in Idaho. Revenue-wise, potatoes
make up the state's largest crop, followed by hay and wheat.

▲ A fly fisherman enjoys the start of the fall season
along the South Fork of the Snake River in eastern Idaho.
Idaho's numerous lakes and rivers, including about ten blue-
ribbon wild trout streams, offer world-class fishing.

▲ The sun rises over the South Fork
of the Snake River in eastern Idaho's Swan Valley.
The river provides fly-fishing for wild trout, while the
nearby Grand Tetons offer winter skiing.

▲ Nature and music lovers enjoy this stand
of aspens in central Idaho's Boulder Mountains.
▶ Big tooth maples begin their color transformation
on a hillside that overlooks the St. Charles Creek drainage.
▶▶ The skeleton of an ancient white pine rises from a rocky
ridge in central Idaho's White Cloud Mountains.

◄ Fishermen angle in the South Fork of the
Boise River, sections of which have excellent populations
of wild rainbow trout, mountain whitefish, and bull trout.
▲ Clean water runs across river rocks in the pristine
ecosystem of the South Fork of the Snake River.

▲ False hellebore *(Veratrum viride)* grows
at the base of an aspen grove in the Clearwater National
Forest. Sometimes confused with skunk cabbage *(Lysichiton americanus),*
false hellebore is a toxic plant, causing sickness and even death if eaten.

▲ The sun warms a couple fly-fishing
in the South Fork of the Boise River. Flowing
approximately seventy-five miles through southwestern
Idaho, the Boise is a tributary of the Snake River.

▲ Ice thaws at Lake Pend Oreille in north
Idaho. It is the state's largest and deepest natural lake.
► The Snake and Salmon rivers meet in Hells Canyon.
►► A storm gathers over the Boise skyline. Both the capital and
the most populous city in the state, Boise received its name from
early French trappers who gave it the French word *boise*,
meaning "wooded," because of the trees in the area.

◄ A summer storm creates an eerie feeing in an
impassable canyon on the Middle Fork of the Salmon River.
▲ Castle Peak, 11,815 feet high, is the tallest
peak in the White Cloud Range.

▲ Horses cross a shallow section of
the Owyhee River. Beginning in Nevada, the
Owyhee flows through Idaho, then into southeastern
Oregon where it empties into the Snake River.

▲ Old-fashioned cowboys drive wild horses
across the dusty Owyhee Desert. The desert covers
some fourteen thousand square miles in northern Nevada,
southwestern Idaho, and southeastern Oregon.

▲ Alpine Creek falls down a granite face and gently
cascades through a high alpine meadow in the Sawtooth Wilderness.
▶ A young couple enjoys rafting on the Middle Fork of the Salmon River.
▶▶ Scott and Shelia Farr drive a horse and buggy across the Thomas
Creek pack bridge on the Middle Fork of the Salmon River.

◄ Summer snow covers rafts at the Boundary
Creek put-in on the Middle Fork of the Salmon River.
▲ Early fall snow outlines the stark rhythmic design of
lodgepole pines in the Gospel-Hump Wilderness.

▲ Yellow Pine Bar glows at dawn on the Main
Salmon River, in the Frank Church Wilderness Area.
► Early frost in the Stanley Basin signals the beginning of
winter. The Stanley Basin is close to the center of Idaho.

◄ Early summer storm clouds reflect magenta
light into the Middle Fork of the Salmon River above
Cow Camp in central Idaho's Frank Church Wilderness.
▲ Lichen covers lava formations in the Gooding City of Rocks.
►► Canola blooms in the Palouse Country of northern Idaho.

▲ A fall thunderstorm illuminates the South
Fork of the Snake River in eastern Idaho's Swan Valley.
▶ Long golden grass blankets the rolling hills of
northern Idaho's Palouse Country.

◄ A yurt glows amber in winter. Though the round shape
of a yurt is copied from those originally created in Central Asia
as temporary shelters for nomads, yurts in the United States are
generally made from hi-tech materials and are not easily moved.
▲ Early winter snow in the Gospel-Hump Wilderness turns fall
foliage to a bright yellow. The wilderness encompasses
more than two hundred thousand acres.

41

▲ Snow covers the high basalt cliff
above Moore's Creek in the Boise National Forest.
▶ In the Boise National Forest, the South Fork of the Payette
River rushes past granite cliffs freshly dusted with snow.

▲ Fall color carpets the floor of a lodgepole pine
grove near Little Redfish Lake in the Sawtooth National Forest.
► A juniper skeleton pokes a hole in the sky in the Devil's Orchard
section of Craters of the Moon National Monument.

◄ Before turning in for the night, rafters enjoy
a campfire at Boise Bar, a popular camp along the
Main Salmon River in Idaho's Frank Church Wilderness.
▲ A mountain biker rides through maples lining
City Creek near Pocatello.

▲ Sumac in fall foliage turns bright red and
yellow. Some varieties of sumac—such as poison oak,
poison ivy, and poison sumac—are poisonous, as their
names indicate. Others have found numerous purposes
from medicinal to the tanning industry to spices
used in Middle Eastern cooking.

▲ Catarafts, inflatable rafts constructed
along the basic principles of a catamaran, move
skillfully through the rocky water of the North
Fork of the Payette River in southern Idaho.

▲ A drift boat successfully runs Tappan
Falls on the famous Middle Fork of the Salmon River.
▶ Paintbrush nestles beneath the Lost River Range. These mountains
include Idaho's highest point, Borah Peak, which rises to 12,662 feet.
▶▶ Indian Creek joins the Middle Fork of the Salmon River in the
Frank Church Wilderness. The Frank Church–River of No
Return Wilderness Area embraces 2.3 million acres.

◄ A young fisherman gets
an assist in reaching dry land.
▲ Fog rises from Stanley Lake in the Sawtooth
Range. The best-known of Idaho's mountain ranges,
the Sawtooths include thirty-three peaks that
are more than ten thousand feet high.

55

▲ The Centennial Mountains form the Continental Divide
and the Idaho-Montana border for more than sixty miles.
▶ Hay figures decorate the landscape near Bellevue,
gateway to the Sawtooth Mountains.

◄ A Chesapeake Bay retriever waits
patiently for his master to call duck in to his
blind in the Snake River Birds of Prey Area near Melba.
▲ A duck hunter sets up decoys in a backwater marsh on
the Snake River upstream from Swan Falls Dam.
►► Shafts of straw break thorough the snow
in the cold Teton Valley.

◄ Bruneau Sand Dunes State Park contains the tallest
single-structured sand dune in North America—470 feet high.
▲ Fall colors fill the slopes of the Teton Basin
near Driggs, in eastern Idaho.

▲ Spring brings rafters to the Lochsa River,
one of north Idaho's famous white-water rivers.
▶ Near the town of McCall in Long Valley, a sparrow has
built her nest in a meadow filled with shooting stars.

◀ Jump Creek Falls tumbles into a catch
basin in the arid Owyhee desert of southern Idaho.
▲ Water rushes past the granite cliffs near the Pistol
Creek Rapid of the Middle Fork of the Salmon River.
▶▶ A rainbow accents the skies above the Middle
Fork of the Salmon River near Jackass camp
in the Frank Church Wilderness.

▲ A mirror image of Elk Peak appears in the hourglass
shape of Kathryn Lake, high in the Sawtooth Wilderness. Elk Peak,
at 10,582 feet high, is one of Idaho's one hundred highest mountains.
▶ Wind and water continue to carve patterns and shapes
into the solid granite rock of City of Rocks.

◄ A red glow appears on the horizon at sunrise above
the Snake River and reflects its brilliance on the land below.
▲ The Snake River cuts through ancient lava in
the Snake River Birds of Prey area.

▲ Mesa Falls cascades over a steep basalt
ledge on the Henrys Fork of the Snake River.
▶ Fall colors line the exposed rocky shoreline of
the South Fork of the Clearwater River.

◄ Fog stripes the Pioneer
Mountains above Wildhorse Creek.
Beaver have dammed up parts of the creek.
▲ Aspen trunks stand tall and strong in a dense grove in the
Caribou-Targhee National Forest. The national forest
encompasses more than three million acres.

◄ Red undergrowth surrounds
granite rock on the shore of the Selway River.
▲ Big tooth maples begin their color transformation in
the St. Charles Creek drainage of eastern Idaho.

▲ The wild and scenic section of the Selway River, in the
heart of the Selway-Bitterroot Wilderness, is one of the premier
river trips in the United States. In order to preserve the isolated,
peaceful atmosphere, only one permit per day is issued during the season.
▶ A tent glows in the Frank Church–River of No Return Wilderness.

◄ Sumac adorns the shoreline of the Snake River in the Hells
Canyon Wilderness Area. The wilderness lies on the Idaho-Oregon border.
▲ Devils club *(Oplopanax horridus),* a thorny plant that annoys hikers and crowds
out other shrubs, thrives beneath a canopy of cedar trees in the Idaho Panhandle.
►► The snowcapped Caribou Peak rises above aspen trees in vibrant
fall color in the Cache National Forest.

▲ Big tooth maple trees contrast with
the lush evergreen forest in the Caribou-Targhee
National Forest, which stretches across southeastern Idaho.
▶ Spring rains turn the rolling hillsides of north Idaho's
Clearwater Country to a rich green.

◄ Bargamin Creek is a major tributary to the
Main Salmon River in the Frank Church Wilderness.
▲ Fog rises as the sun burns off the cloud cover in the Clearwater
National Forest. The national forest covers nearly two million acres,
stretching from the jagged peaks of the Bitterroot Mountains in the east to
the river canyons and rolling hills of the Palouse Prairie in the west.

89

▲ Arnica, paintbrush, and showy
daisies bloom in the Seven Devils Range.
▶ The skeletal remains of a pine tree sit atop a
rocky rise in the Hells Canyon Wilderness.
▶▶ Sunrise illuminates the tops of the
granite canyons of City of Rocks.

◄ The DeVote Memorial Grove, situated along the
Lochsa River, is home to ancient cedar trees. The Lochsa
originates in the Bitterroot Mountains on the Montana border.
▲ Aspens turn yellow in the cool September temperatures
of the Stanley Basin. The aspens' color change
signals the coming of winter.

▲ Fall colors line the shores of Medicine Lake in
the Coeur d'Alene National Forest. The Coeur d'Alene,
Kaniksu, and St. Joe national forests together make
up the Idaho Panhandle National Forest.

▲ A change of seasons is on display across
the riverbanks of the North Fork of the Payette River.
The river is named for François Payette, a French-Canadian
fur trapper who settled in the area in the early 1800s.

▲ Fog rises from a pool of
still water in the Sawtooth National Forest.
▶ Bear grass blooms near Ship Island Lake in the Big
Horn Crags of the Frank Church Wilderness Area.

▲ Ice forms around colorful rocks
along the St. Joseph River, known locally simply as
the St. Joe. Located in the Idaho Panhandle, the St. Joe is
known not only for its great fly-fishing but also for its beauty.
▶ French Creek, in southwestern Idaho, is a tributary
to the main Salmon River.

◄ Waders hang from the porch of a cabin at
the Whitewater Ranch, located on the Salmon River.
▲ A fly fisherman casts in the fog on the
South Fork of the Boise River.

▲ Green rolling fields are interspersed with
pine groves in north Idaho's classic Palouse Country.
► Mountain asters thrive on the hillside in Chamberlain Basin
in the oval-shaped White Cloud Mountain Range.

◄ In the Sawtooth Wilderness, fiery light reflects from
high clouds, appearing to set the upper Cramer Lake on fire.
▲ Elephant head *(Pedicularis groenlandica)* blooms on Meadow
Creek in the Sawtooth Wilderness Area of central Idaho.
►► Fall Creek Falls tumbles into the South Fork of
the Snake River in eastern Idaho's Swan Valley.

107

▲ Lupine and paintbrush dot the area
beneath the Lost River Range near Mackay.
▶ Lupine and balsamroot bloom in the Sun
Valley foothills leading to Mount Baldy.
▶▶ Sawtooth Peaks reflect in Twin
Lake in the Sawtooth Wilderness.